THOMAS PAINE
and His Common Sense

Author and Thinker

AMERICAN REVOLUTION | GRADE 4 BIOGRAPHY | CHILDREN'S BIOGRAPHIES

DISSECTED LIVES
auto biographies

First Edition, 2020

Published in the United States by Speedy Publishing LLC, 40 E Main Street, Newark, Delaware 19711 USA.

© 2020 Dissected Lives Books, an imprint of Speedy Publishing LLC

All rights reserved.

Without limiting the rights under the copyright reserved above, no part of this publication may be reproduced, stored in or introduced into a retrieval system, or transmitted, in any form, or by any means (electronic, mechanical, photocopying, recording, or otherwise), without the prior written permission of the copyright owner.

All images in this book have been reproduced with the knowledge and prior consent of the artists concerned, and no responsibility is accepted by producer, publisher, or printer for any infringement of copyright or otherwise arising from the contents of this publication.

Dissected Lives Books are available at special discounts when purchased in bulk for industrial and sales-promotional use. For details contact our Special Sales Team at Speedy Publishing LLC, 40 E Main Street, Newark, Delaware 19711 USA. Telephone (888) 248-4521 Fax: (210) 519-4043.

10 9 8 7 6 * 5 4 3 2 1

Print Edition: 9781541950788
Digital Edition: 9781541952584
Hardcover Edition: 9781541976894

See the world in pictures. Build your knowledge in style.
www.speedypublishing.com

TABLE OF CONTENTS

Thomas Paine, the Englishman 7
Thomas Paine, Coming to America 17
Thomas Paine, Magazine Editor 23
Thomas Paine's "Common Sense" 29
The Popularity of "Common Sense" 35
Thomas Paine's "The American Crisis" 41
Thomas Paine's "Public Good" 49
Thomas Paine and the "Rights of Man" 55
Thomas Paine and "The Age of Reason" 61
Back to America 67
Summary 75

THOMAS PAINE

Thomas Paine was unlike many of the other important figures of the American Revolutionary War in that he was not born and raised in the American colonies. He left England as an adult after befriending Benjamin Franklin, but soon made his mark on the people living in the colonies. He authored several significant political essays, but his pamphlet, "Common Sense", was one of the most influential writings pushing the colonists toward war for their independence against the British. Let's look at the life of Thomas Paine and this influential writing.

Thomas Paine, the Englishman

PAINE WAS EDUCATED AT THETFORD GRAMMAR SCHOOL IN THETFORD, NORFOLK, ENGLAND.

In 1737, Thomas Paine was born in Thetford, England. As a child, he attended school sporadically...just enough to learn to read and write. Despite this, he later proved to be an excellent writer. Life in England was not good for Paine.

Starting at age 13, he worked long, hard hours alongside his father making rope stays for merchant vessels. After that, he took a job in the **excise**[1] department as a tax collector. While working in the excise office, he penned his first published political essay, an article calling for higher pay for excise workers. His outspokenness got him fired.

---

[1] Excise – A tax on specific things, like tobacco.

Paine then started a tobacco shop business, but it went bankrupt. He was forced to sell most of his belongings to avoid going to debtor's prison. He was a failure as a business owner. In fact, he failed at almost every job he had in England. His personal life was also marked with tragedy.

PAINE MARRIED A SECOND TIME AND HIS WIFE LEFT HIM.

In 1760, Paine lost both his wife and child in childbirth. He married a second time and his wife left him. His future looked dismal...until he met an American named Benjamin Franklin.

Thomas Paine, Coming to America

Benjamin Franklin, who was visiting London, read Thomas Paine's published essay on excise workers and liked what he read. When Franklin inquired about the author of the piece, the Commission of the Excise, George Lewis Scott, took him to meet Thomas Paine. A friendship blossomed. Franklin persuaded Paine to leave his home in England and move to America. He even gave him letters of introduction to help him secure employment in publishing.

BENJAMIN FRANKLIN

PAINE NEARLY PERISHED ON THE VOYAGE ACROSS THE ATLANTIC.

Paine nearly perished on the voyage across the Atlantic. Typhoid fever swept through the ship, killing five passengers. When he arrived in Philadelphia on November 30, 1774, he was so sick and weak that a doctor had to carry him off the ship. He spent a month and a half recovering from his illness and regaining his strength. Once he did, he was ready to make his mark in the New World.

Thomas Paine, Magazine Editor

Thomas Paine took the position of editor of the *Pennsylvania Magazine* in March of 1775. Finally, he had found a job that he loved. He excelled at writing and publishing. He had a knack for writing about political and social causes. Under a pen name, he published an article, titled "African Slavery in America", in which he condemned the African slave trade and the practice of slavery in general.

PAINE CONDEMNED THE AFRICAN SLAVE TRADE AND THE PRACTICE OF SLAVERY IN GENERAL.

He soon took up other causes as well. The American colonies were on the brink of war with England over a series of injustices and Paine felt compelled to write about them. At a time when tensions were high between the colonists and the English, Paine's writings helped to fan the flames of **discontent**².

² Discontent – Dissatisfaction.

Thomas Paine's "Common Sense"

Thomas Paine quickly adapted to life as an American. When the British and colonists clashed in battle in Lexington and Concord on April 19, 1775, Paine staunchly supported his new homeland.

He believed that the colonists should do more than revolt against taxation without representation...he felt that they should seek their independence from the British.

THE BATTLE OF LEXINGTON

He detailed his ideas in a fifty-page essay that he printed in a pamphlet called "Common Sense" on January 10, 1776. Paine laid out his argument in a clear and compelling manner that led his readers to the obvious conclusion that the American colonies must rid themselves of British rule.

PHILADELPHIA SITE WHERE THE FIRST EDITION OF PAINE'S COMMON SENSE WAS PRINTED.

TITLE PAGE OF THE PAMPHLET "COMMON SENSE" BY THOMAS PAINE, PUBLISHED IN 1776.

COMMON SENSE;

ADDRESSED TO THE

INHABITANTS

OF

AMERICA,

On the following interesting

SUBJECTS.

I. Of the Origin and Design of Government in general, with concise Remarks on the English Constitution.
II. Of Monarchy and Hereditary Succession.
III. Thoughts on the present State of American Affairs.
IV. Of the present Ability of America, with some miscellaneous Reflections.

Man knows no Master save creating HEAVEN,
Or those whom choice and common good ordain.
THOMSON.

PHILADELPHIA;
Printed, and Sold, by R. BELL, in Third
MDCCLXXVI

The Popularity of "Common Sense"

At the time of the publication of "Common Sense", revolution was not on everyone's minds. In fact, most colonists wanted to stay under British governance, even though they were unhappy with the taxes levied upon them by the British. "Common Sense" was read and reread by these undecided colonists. The pamphlet was then passed on to others. In many areas, it was read aloud before a town meeting or other group gathering.

Unlike other political writings of the era, Paine wrote "Common Sense" using plain, easy-to-understand language without Latin phrasings and confusing philosophical debates. The words resonated with people. They followed the logic Paine outlined in the pamphlet and reached the same conclusion as him. Paine sold more than 500,000 copies of "Common Sense", making it one of the most popular and influential political texts of the Revolutionary War era.

PAINE WROTE "COMMON SENSE" USING PLAIN, EASY-TO-UNDERSTAND LANGUAGE WITHOUT LATIN PHRASINGS AND CONFUSING PHILOSOPHICAL DEBATES.

Thomas Paine's "The American Crisis"

Thomas Paine published another important persuasive pamphlet at the end of 1776. Called "The American Crisis", the work began with the now-famous line, "These are the times that try men's souls."

The *American Crisis.*

NUMBER I.

By the Author of COMMON SENSE.

THESE are the times that try men's souls: The summer soldier and the sunshine patriot will, in this crisis, shrink from the service of his country; but he that stands it NOW, deserves the love and thanks of man and woman. Tyranny, like hell, is not easily conquered; yet we have this consolation with us, that the harder the conflict, the more glorious the triumph. What we obtain too cheap, we esteem too lightly:—'Tis dearness only that gives every thing its value. Heaven knows how to set a proper price upon its goods; and it would be strange, indeed, if so celestial an article as FREEDOM should not be highly rated. Britain, with an army to enforce her tyranny, has declared, that she has a right (*not only to* TAX, *but*) "to BIND *us in* ALL CASES WHATSOEVER," and if being bound in that manner is not slavery, then is there not such a thing as slavery upon earth. Even the expression is impious, for so unlimited a power can belong only to GOD.

WHETHER the Independence of the Continent was declared too soon, or delayed too long, I will not now enter into as an argument; my own simple opinion is, that had it been eight months earlier, it would have been much better. We did not make a proper use of last winter, neither could we, while we were in a dependent state. However, the fault, if it were one, was all our own; we have none to blame but ourselves*. But no great deal is lost yet; all that Howe has been doing for this month past is rather a ravage than a conquest, which the spirit of the Jersies a year ago would have quickly repulsed, and which time and a little resolution will soon recover.

THE FIRST PAGE FROM "THE THE AMERICAN CRISIS," A PAMPHLET AUTHORED BY THOMAS PAINE.

PAINE'S WORK WAS WRITTEN TO BOLSTER THE LAGGING SPIRITS OF THE CONTINENTAL ARMY.

This work was written to bolster the lagging spirits of the Continental Army in the face of a series of defeats against the better-trained and better-armed British. He wrote of the Americans as being on the side of goodness and virtue against a bitter enemy.

During the Winter of 1776, General George Washington read "The American Crisis" to his troops who were wintering over at Valley Forge. Moral was low as the men struggled against disease, frigid cold, and inadequate supplies. General Washington used Paine's words to motivate his men and help them to understand the just cause they were fighting for. Paine expanded on "The American Crisis" by launching a series of similar-themed pamphlets, numbering 1 through 16.

TROOPS OF THE CONTINENTAL ARMY CAMPED AT VALLEY FORGE DURING THE WINTER OF 1776.

Thomas Paine's "Public Good"

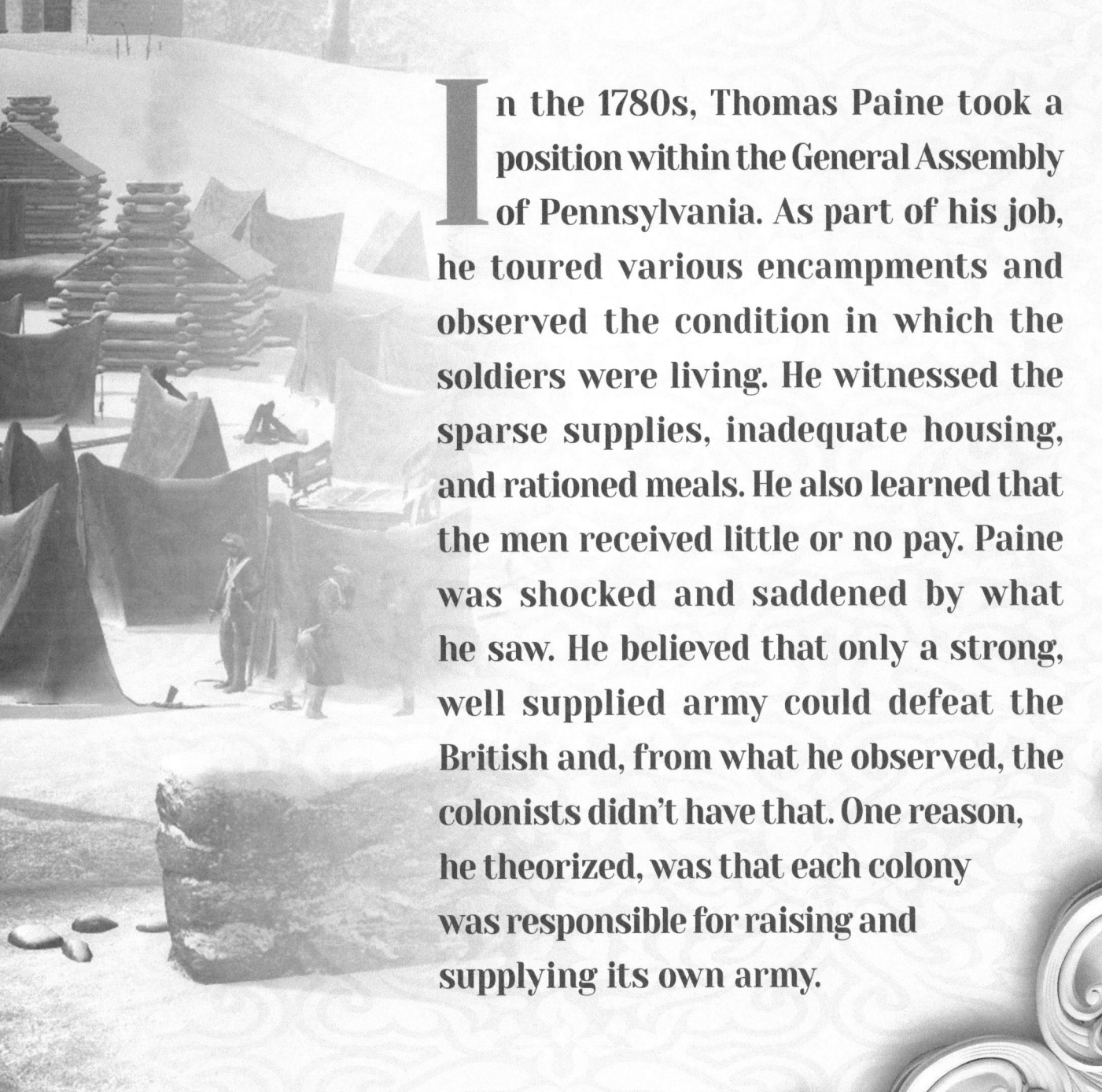

In the 1780s, Thomas Paine took a position within the General Assembly of Pennsylvania. As part of his job, he toured various encampments and observed the condition in which the soldiers were living. He witnessed the sparse supplies, inadequate housing, and rationed meals. He also learned that the men received little or no pay. Paine was shocked and saddened by what he saw. He believed that only a strong, well supplied army could defeat the British and, from what he observed, the colonists didn't have that. One reason, he theorized, was that each colony was responsible for raising and supplying its own army.

PUBLIC GOOD,

BEING

AN EXAMINATION

Into the Claim of Virginia to the

VACANT WESTERN TERRITORY,

AND

OF THE RIGHT OF

The United States to the Same.

TO WHICH IS ADDED,

Proposals for laying off a new State,

TO BE APPLIED AS A FUND FOR CARRYING ON THE WAR, OR REDEEMING THE NATIONAL DEBT.

BY THE AUTHOR OF COMMON SENSE.

PHILADELPHIA:
ed by JOHN DUNLAP, in Market-street.
M,DCC,LXXX.

TITLE PAGE OF THE PAMPHLET, "PUBLIC GOOD" BY THOMAS PAINE

In his 1780 pamphlet, "Public Good", he supported the Continental Congress's idea for a strong central government that oversees the individual states. Paine noted that it was for the good of the public for states to share resources so that a well-supplied national army could defend the country.

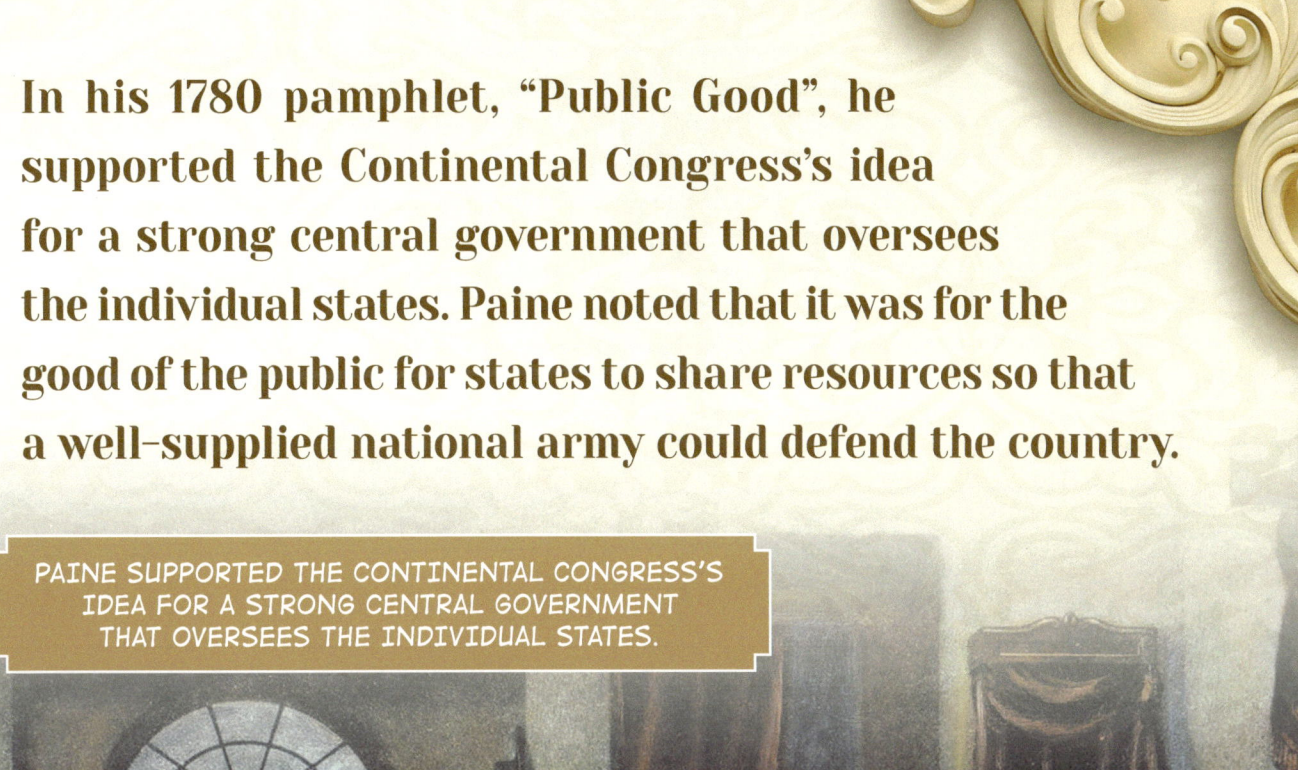

PAINE SUPPORTED THE CONTINENTAL CONGRESS'S IDEA FOR A STRONG CENTRAL GOVERNMENT THAT OVERSEES THE INDIVIDUAL STATES.

Thomas Paine and the "Rights of Man"

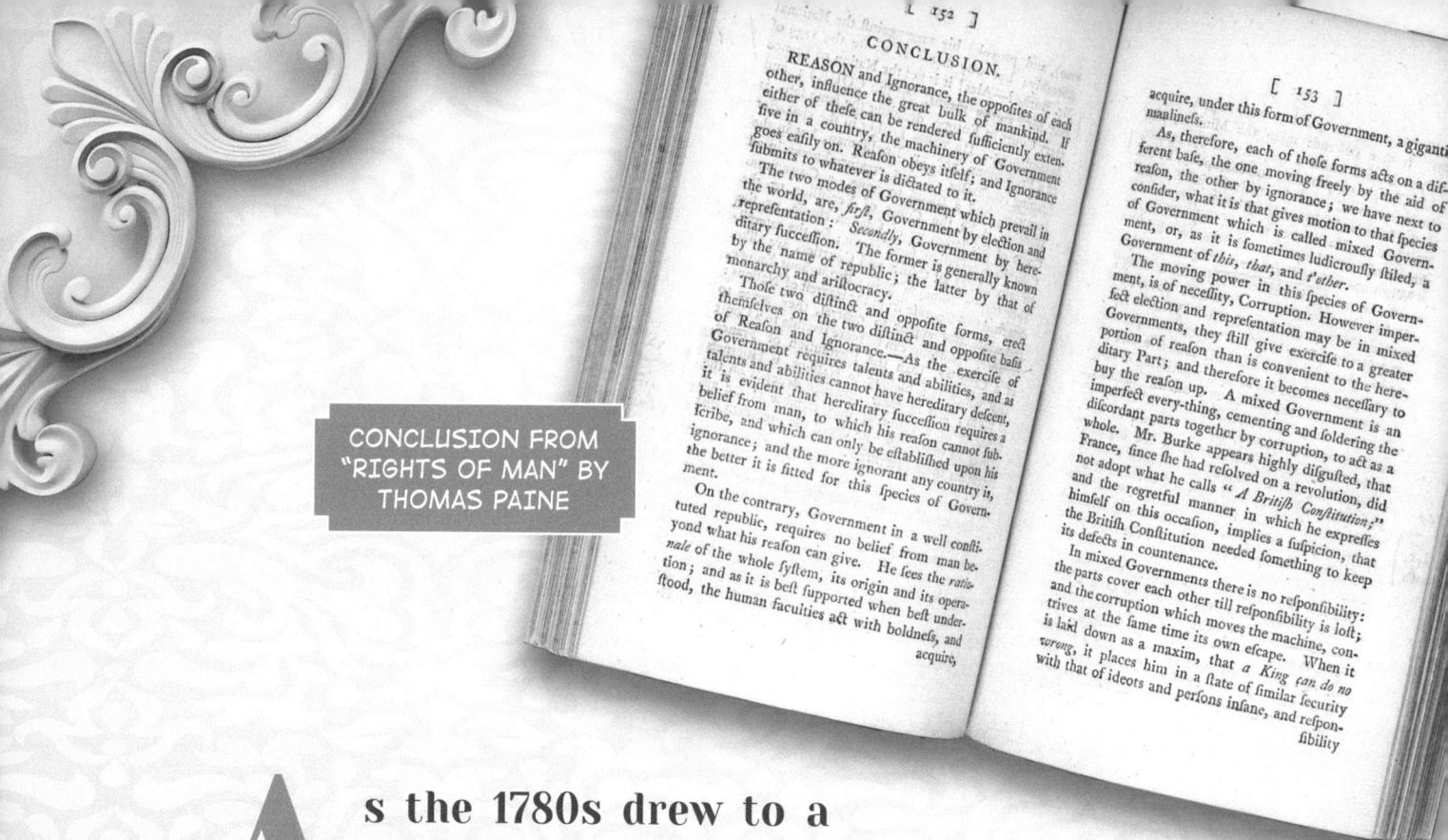

CONCLUSION FROM "RIGHTS OF MAN" BY THOMAS PAINE

As the 1780s drew to a close, Thomas Paine left America and returned to England. There, he learned about the French Revolution, mainly from Edmund Burke's written condemnation of it, published in 1790. Paine was moved to pen a written response to Burke's work in which he outlined his reasons for supporting the French Revolution.

THOMAS PAINE RELEASED "RIGHTS OF MAN" IN 1971.

The result was the 1791 "Rights of Man". In this book, Paine called for the end to the traditional **aristocratic**[3] rules across all of Europe that favored the wealthy elite at the expense of the average worker. Paine also wrote harshly about inheritance laws. "Rights of Man" so upset the British government that the book was banned, and an arrest decree went out for Paine on charges of treason. By this time, Paine was on his way to France, so he avoided arrest.

---

[3] Aristocratic – Associated with the noble or ruling class.

Thomas Paine and "The Age of Reason"

In France, Thomas Paine continued to advocate for revolution in France. He pushed for banishing the ousted King Louis XVI rather than see him executed. Paine's effort landed him in prison for nearly a year in 1794.

SEVERAL EARLY COPIES OF "THE AGE OF REASON" BY THOMAS PAINE HELD BY THE CENTER FOR INQUIRY LIBRARY, RARE BOOK ROOM, IN AMHERST, NEW YORK.

During his incarceration, Paine wrote part one of his "The Age of Reason". This book shed a spotlight on religious corruption and how religion was used for political gain. He even went so far as to question the Bible's validity. Like "Rights of Man", "The Age of Reason" was **controversial**[4] and disrupted conventional thought. "The Age of Reason" was also banned in England and the British government pressed charges against people who sold or distributed it.

---

[4] Controversial – Something that caused public debate or dispute.

Back to America

Thomas Paine remained in France after he was released from jail. He spent his time writing two more parts to his "The Age of Reason", which he also published.

THOMAS PAINE LIVED AT THE LIBRAIRIE GUÉNÉGAUD, A LEFT BANK BOOKSHOP IN PARIS FROM 1798 UNTIL 1802.

In 1802, Paine returned to the United States at the invitation of Thomas Jefferson. He continued with his political writing upon his return to the United States, addressing social and political injustices.

Thomas Paine died at the age of 72 on June 8, 1809 at his home in New York City. He has been remembered for his role in the American Revolutionary War through his controversial and influential writing.

ENTRANCE TO THOMAS PAINE COTTAGE IN NEW ROCHELLE, NEW YORK

THOMAS PAINE BURIAL SITE IN NEW ROCHELLE, NEW YORK

ON THIS SITE WAS BURIED
THOMAS PAINE
1737 — 1809
AUTHOR OF
COMMON SENSE
THE PAMPHLET THAT STIRRED
THE AMERICAN COLONIES TO INDEPENDENCE

JOHN ADAMS said:
"Without the pen of Paine the sword of Washington would have been wielded in vain"
AND
"History is to ascribe the American Revolution to Thomas Paine."

DONATED BY ROWENA STILLMAN IN THE
175TH YEAR OF THE AMERICAN REPUBLIC

Summary

Although Thomas Paine did not start life as an American, he played a key role in rousing the colonists to demand independence from the British. With little formal education, Paine was able to write in an informative and persuasive manner, evoking passion and anger in his readers. His "Common Sense" laid out the case for American independence, while his other writings addressed other political and social concerns. During his life, Paine lived in England, the United States, and France, but seemed to find his greatest success as an editor and writer in the U.S. His name is forever linked with "Common Sense".

Made in the USA
Columbia, SC
31 March 2025